D1442033

# Discovering Mission Santa Inés

## BY SOFIA NUÑES

Cavendish
Square

New York

Published in 2015 by Cavendish Square Publishing, LLC
243 5th Avenue, Suite 136, New York, NY 10016

Website: cavendishsq.com

This publication represents the opinions and views of the author based on his or her personal experience, knowledge, and research. The information in this book serves as a general guide only. The author and publisher have used their best efforts in preparing this book and disclaim liability rising directly or indirectly from the use and application of this book.

CPSIA Compliance Information: Batch #WS14CSQ

All websites were available and accurate when this book was sent to press.

Library of Congress Cataloging-in-Publication Data

Nuñes, Sofía
Discovering Mission Santa Inés / Sofia Nuñes.
pages cm. — (California missions)
Includes index.
ISBN 978-1-62713-097-4 (hardcover) ISBN 978-1-62713-099-8 (ebook)
1. Santa Inés Mission (Solvang, Calif.)—History—Juvenile literature. 2. Spanish mission buildings—California—Solvang—History—Juvenile literature. 3. Franciscans—California—Solvang—History—Juvenile literature. 4. Chumash Indians—Missions—California—Solvang—History—Juvenile literature. 5. California—History—To 1846—Juvenile literature. I. Title.

F869.S487N85 2015
979.4'91—dc23

2014007202

Editorial Director: Dean Miller
Editor: Kristen Susienka
Copy Editor: Cynthia Roby
Art Director: Jeffrey Talbot
Designer: Douglas Brooks
Photo Researcher: J8 Media
Production Manager: Jennifer Ryder-Talbot
Production Editor: David McNamara

The photographs in this book are used by permission and through the courtesy of: Cover photo by Stephen Saks/Lonely Planet Images/Getty Images; Witold Skrypczak/Lonely Planet Images/Getty Images, 1; Richard Cummins/Lonely Planet Images/Getty Images, 4; De Agostini/A. Dagli Orti/Getty Images, 6; Marilyn Angel Wynn/Nativestock/Getty Images, 7; © Ann Thiermann, 8–9; Courtesy of UC Berkeley, Bancroft Library, 10; © 1998 Kayte Deioma, 11; Science & Society Picture Library/SSPL/Getty Images, 12; © 2014 Pentacle Press, 13; Howcheng/File:Smaller Junipero Serra statue, Mission San Buenaventura.JPG/Wikimedia Commons, 14; Francisco de Zurbarán/File:Francisco de Zurbarán - Santa Inés.jpg/Wikimedia Commons, 16; © Pentacle Press, 18; Courtesy CMRC, 20; © Pentacle Press, 24–25; Junkyardsparkle/File:Joseph John Chapman and Gaudalupe Ortega y Sánchez c1847.jpg/Wikimedia Commons, 27; © Pentacle Press, 29; Courtesy of UC Berkeley, Bancroft Library, 32–33; Library of Congress Prints and Photographs Division, 34; Witold Skrypczak/Lonely Planet Images/Getty Images, 41.

Printed in the United States of America

# Contents

Mission Santa Inés was one of the last missions built in California.

# 1
# Explorers in California

In the city of Solvang, California stands Mission Santa Inés. The structure is a living relic to the mission system that once dominated the West Coast, bringing settlers, **friars**, and new ideas to the land. Santa Inés was the nineteenth of twenty-one missions that covered *Alta*, or "upper," California. Its history is vast, filled with triumphs and trials, and testifies to a new era in the life of the land of California.

## THE SPANISH EMPIRE

The sixteenth century was a time of exploration for many European countries. At its forefront was Spain, a country with much power over the rest of the known world at that time. Spanish **conquistadors** explored a vast area of the Americas throughout the 1500s, searching for new riches or a new way of life. It was there that they encountered the Native people and their supposed wealth. These men were following in the footsteps of Christopher Columbus, who had accidentally "discovered" the New World (South, Central, and North America) on an expedition for Spain in 1492. Over decades, the Spanish **empire** in the Americas spread from the southwest desert of North America to the Andes

In the 1500s, **Hernán Cortés** and other conquistadors traveled to the Americas to claim land for Spain.

Mountains in South America. This empire was called New Spain. Everywhere the Spanish **colonists** went, they spread Spanish culture and the Christian religion.

In 1542, the Spanish claimed California. This was the last territory on the borders of the empire to become part of New Spain. At the time, "California" consisted of what are now California and the Baja Peninsula of Mexico. It was divided into two parts, Alta California and *Baja*, or "lower," California.

By the 1760s, however, Spain still had not built any **settlements** in Alta California. There were many reasons the Spaniards had not built communities there. No riches and no direct water route through America are two examples.

In 1768, Spain learned that the Russians and the English wanted to settle in Alta California. Russian explorers and fur traders had established colonies in Alaska and were moving farther south along the coast. Whoever controlled the coast could control trade routes across the Pacific Ocean. The Spanish government was afraid to lose this important territory to the Russians. They decided to take action.

The Spanish planned to build a chain of missions along the coast of Alta California. They would send Spanish friars to convert the Native people, with soldiers nearby to protect them. By that time, Spain had already built missions outside of Alta California because they thought it was a good way to settle a new land.

# 2
# The Chumash

When the Spanish first arrived in Alta California, there were already many Native American tribes living there. More than 100 different groups, each with its own language or **dialect**, territory, and identity, occupied the land. The Native people living near Mission Santa Inés were known as the Chumash.

## PEOPLE OF THE COAST

The Chumash tribe once lived all along the Southern California coastline. Because they were so dominant and thought to be the oldest tribe in California, they called themselves the First People. They were generally a nonviolent people who loved music, making it part of their everyday lives. They sang songs for celebrations, such as the birth of a baby, and for healing, hunting, warfare, and harvesting.

**This is a Chumash tomol spirit boat, carved with designs that came from dreams.**

**The Chumash lived in thriving villages throughout California. Each village had many families living in it, and each person helped the community survive.**

Their musical instruments included rattles made from turtle shells, whistles carved from wood and the bones of birds, and string instruments similar to the hunting bow.

The Chumash were also skilled craftspeople. They made fine baskets for storage, offerings, and gifts. Other tribes often made blankets from animal fur, but the Chumash people were known to weave feathers into the beautiful blankets that they made. Later, at Mission Santa Inés, the Chumash would use their skills to great success.

## CHUMASH HOUSING AND TRANSPORTATION

The Chumash lived in dome-shaped houses that were usually quite large. Some housed up to four families, while others were

home to up to fifty people. Sycamore poles or willow branches were used as frames for these houses. Whale ribs were used to build the doorways.

Canoes, called *tomols* in Chumash, were as important to the coastal Chumash as horses were to the Native people of the Plains. They built their canoes from wood they brought down from the mountains. These canoes, which were used mostly for fishing, could hold twelve to twenty people, and were very important vessels for catching fish.

## HUNTERS AND GATHERERS

In addition to fish, the Chumash hunted game and gathered berries, seeds, and nuts. Hunting and gathering had always been

**Many Native groups, including the Chumash, fished and hunted to get food.**

the way Native people survived, but these methods did not always provide a steady source of food. Sometimes the tribe would go hungry. The Chumash, like other Native groups, lived in harmony with nature, eating whatever was available in the wild. They did not farm or raise cattle, cut down forests, or kill entire animal populations.

The only gardening done by the first California people was growing tobacco—which was smoked, chewed, and eaten. It was also used by the *shamans*—healers believed to have special powers—in their ceremonies to cure the sick.

## CEREMONIES

Ceremonies played an important part in the lives of the Native people. As hunter-gatherers, the Chumash lived close to nature, so their ceremonies marked important times of the year. This included harvest time, the winter solstice, and the return of spring. They used **amulets**, made from painted stones, for luck in fishing and hunting trips. These stones were also used by the shamans. The shaman was an important person in a tribe because it was thought that he or she communicated between humans and the spirit world. Some Native American tribes cremated their dead, but the Chumash held burials for most of their members, the exception being people of high importance.

The Chumash also created drawings and paintings, called pictographs, on the walls of caves around where they lived. The pictographs told stories of their lifestyle and beliefs. The earliest paintings were black, but over time they were painted with more colors, made from different rocks and minerals. Charcoal was used to make black paint, and the mineral hematite made red. Today, these drawings can still be seen in the Santa Ynez Mountains.

**Today the Santa Inez Chumash carry on the traditions of their ancestors.**

# 3
# The
# Mission System

In the eyes of the missionaries, the main goal of the missions was to **convert** the local people to Christianity. The Europeans who encountered the Native populations considered them pagans, or non-Christians, for they did not share the same religious beliefs or traditions as the Spanish. They also led freer lifestyles, wore little or no clothing, and did not farm or live in reliable homes. Therefore, the Spanish king and church leaders believed it was their God-given duty to convert the Native people, as well as to protect them. Once converted, the Native people were supposed to perform Christian work by building mission structures and raising crops and livestock. The missions were meant to act as homes and "civilized" institutions that would train the Native people to become Spanish citizens. However, rather than improve the lives of the people they affected, the mission system damaged a thriving culture and way of life that had been celebrated for thousands of years.

**The sixteenth-century arrival of the Spanish would eventually damage Native culture.**

# ALTA CALIFORNIA'S MISSION SYSTEM

The Spaniards built twenty-one missions along the coast of California over fifty-four years. Mission San Diego de Alcalá, the first mission, was founded in 1769. The founder of the Alta California missions was Fray Junípero Serra. Since he had converted many Native people at missions set up previously in Baja California, he was chosen to found and manage the Alta California missions. Mission San Francisco Solano, the last mission, was founded in 1823. When all the missions were constructed, they were about a day's ride apart from each other and located on the best farming lands. Combined, they formed

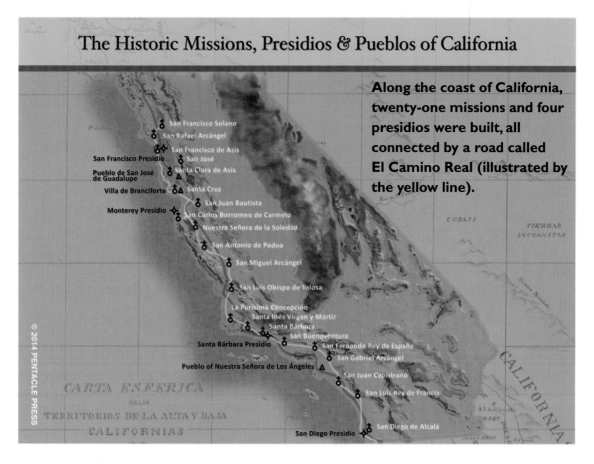

### The Historic Missions, Presidios & Pueblos of California

Along the coast of California, twenty-one missions and four presidios were built, all connected by a road called El Camino Real (illustrated by the yellow line).

San Francisco Solano
San Rafael Arcángel
San Francisco de Asis
San Francisco Presidio — San José
Pueblo de San José de Guadalupe — Santa Clara de Asis
Villa de Branciforte — Santa Cruz
San Juan Bautista
Monterey Presidio — San Carlos Borromeo de Carmelo
Nuestra Señora de la Soledad
San Antonio de Padua
San Miguel Arcángel
San Luis Obispo de Tolosa
La Purísima Concepción
Santa Inés Virgen y Mártir
Santa Bárbara
San Buenaventura
Santa Bárbara Presidio — San Fernando Rey de España
Pueblo of Nuestra Señora de Los Ángeles — San Gabriel Arcángel
San Juan Capistrano
San Luis Rey de Francia
San Diego Presidio — San Diego de Alcalá

© 2014 PENTACLE PRESS

**Fray Junípero Serra was the first leader of the Alta California missions.**

a chain up the California coast, following a road called *El Camino Real*. This road granted travelers safe passage from one mission to another. Small towns, called *pueblos*, eventually grew near or around the missions. The mission communities traded crops, cattle, and other goods with the people in the towns.

All twenty-one missions housed hundreds of Native people who had converted to Christianity. These **neophytes**, or newly converted people, had to follow strict rules given by the friar (*fray* in Spanish) in charge. It was not always easy, and some people were punished for not doing what they were told. The missionaries thought that once the neophytes learned Spanish ways and customs, they could return the land to them to manage. Unfortunately, that did not happen. The mission system would change the lives of Native people forever.

# 4
# Founding the Mission

When the mission friars asked the Spanish government to build a new mission, there were already eighteen missions in Alta California. Most of the missions were located about a day's ride apart, on El Camino Real. The reason for a new mission was simple: two of the missions, Santa Bárbara and La Purísima Concepción, were too far apart. Many Native families lived in between them. The friars of New Spain wanted to build an inland mission located closer to Santa Bárbara and La Purísima Concepción so that they could convert the families living nearby to Christianity. A new mission would also expand the amount of territory that belonged to Spain.

## FINDING A GOOD AREA

Fray Estévan Tápis, head (or president) of the missions since 1803, had gone in search of a good location for the new mission in 1798. He was accompanied by experienced soldiers who had been exploring other parts of California. Initially, two sites were selected as possible locations for the new mission. First was a Native village, or *ranchería*, called Calahuasa. A mission at that location could minister to the Native population while also providing a buffer to a hostile Native group called the Tulares, who lived to the north.

The second option was a place on a high knoll next to the Santa Ynez River. The governor at that time had died, and his successor, José de Arrillaga, wanted to investigate both sites before making a decision. In the end, he chose the location at Santa Ynez. It was a beautiful place, surrounded by oak-covered

**Mission Santa Inés was named after Saint Agnes, a young girl martyred in the fourth century.**

mountains. The Chumash called it *Alajulapa*, meaning "corner." Here, the land supplied trees for lumber, good soil for growing crops, and plenty of fresh water for drinking. Everything the missionaries needed for survival was there and available.

Fray Tápis arrived at the site in 1804 with several soldiers and neophytes from missions Santa Bárbara and La Purísima Concepción. During that time, there was a small group of Native people who wanted the missionaries to leave the area, and so they hurt and even killed settlers in regions near to the other missions. The soldiers would help with running and building Mission Santa Inés as well as protecting it from any attacks. Before the official dedication, over the course of six months, the friars, soldiers, and neophytes built various buildings. They also constructed a shelter from brushwood for the founding ceremonies.

On September 17, 1804, Mission Santa Inés became the nineteenth mission in California. Fray Tápis celebrated the first Mass, or religious ceremony, with the help of Frays Marcelino Ciprés, José Antonio Calzada, and José Romualdo Gutierrez. This ceremony confirmed that the mission established there was first for God and that it also belonged to Spain. Amazingly, nearly 200 Chumash attended. They were curious to see what the Spanish were doing on the land. That day, friars baptized twenty-seven Native children. Additionally, fifteen Chumash adults expressed interest in learning about Catholicism.

Most missions were dedicated to saints of the Catholic Church. This one was dedicated to Saint Agnes, a Christian **martyr**. Saint Agnes lived in fourth-century Rome. She was put to death at the age of thirteen because she refused to give up her Christian faith. Legend holds that she restored the sight of a blind man by praying. She is still one of the most popular Christian saints.

# THE POPULATION GROWS

The families of the twenty-seven baptized children became members of Mission Santa Inés. Their baptism into the Christian faith allowed them to live at the mission. Many members of the families and the Chumash tribe helped build the mission church and the other buildings. By the end of the first year, 112 Chumash had converted to Christianity. A total of 570 neophytes, both from other missions and the surrounding Chumash population, were living at Mission Santa Inés.

# FRAYS TÁPIS, CALZADA, AND GUTIERREZ

Santa Inés was the only mission founded by Fray Tápis. He was known for his musical talents and for teaching the neophytes to sing and play instruments that were new to them. As president of the missions after Fermín Francisco de Lasuén (the second mission president), Fray Tápis did not stay to run the affairs of Mission Santa Inés. It was Fray Calzada and Fray Gutierrez who took on the task as the mission's first resident friars. Fray Calzada and Fray Gutierrez were hardworking men who believed in building sturdy structures at the mission. They taught the laborers to make **adobe** dwellings and ways to farm certain crops.

Fray Calzada was at the mission until his death in 1814. Over the years, Mission Santa Inés would come under the guidance of ten more friars. Some of them died and were buried in the church at the mission.

**At each mission, friars instructed men, women, and children how to build and take care of the mission.**

# 5
# Early Days at Mission Santa Inés

Soon after founding Mission Santa Inés, the soldiers and neophytes started constructing permanent buildings. These structures were made of adobe with **thatched** roofs. Adobe, which was used throughout the mission buildings, is sun-dried brick made of soil, water, and straw. The buildings resembled the first structures that had been built prior to the mission's dedication. By the end of 1806, there were several buildings on the mission site, including a temporary church; a sacristy, where holy objects were kept; a granary, where grain was stored; and living space for Frays Calzada and Gutierrez. There were also adobe huts with doors and windows for the neophyte families, a blacksmith shop, rooms for weaving and basket making, and a guardhouse.

## SKILLS AND CROPS

Although Mission Santa Inés was smaller than the other missions, it was a major producer of goods. The friars taught the neophytes many trades and also allowed them to continue to put their own skills to use at the mission. The community of friars and neophytes grew several crops, such as wheat, barley, corn, and beans. Throughout the mission's existence, its numbers of livestock increased. This included cattle, sheep, horses, mules, and pigs. The mission warehouse was filled with the many types of goods made there, including animal hides, tallow for candles and soap, cloth woven from wool, and dairy products. The neophytes learned to make beautiful saddles decorated with silver. Because of the skill of the neophytes, the mission became known for its leather and metal products.

## EARTHQUAKE OF 1812

Most of Mission Santa Inés's buildings were completed in the early 1800s. However, these structures did not remain intact for long. In 1812 a strong earthquake struck the mission. It destroyed

**The earthquake that struck Mission Santa Inés in 1812 damaged many buildings, including the mill. Its ruins are seen here.**

the church and caused serious damage to the other buildings. The friars were determined to rebuild. By 1813, a *monjerío,* or living quarters for unmarried girls, was completed, as was another granary, which was used as a temporary place of worship until the new church could be built. Construction on the new church did not begin until 1814.

On July 4, 1817, the mission community celebrated the completion of the new church. The three bells in the tower rang on that day. It had taken two years to complete the outside of the church. The adobe walls were built 5 to 6 feet (1.5 to 1.8 meters) thick to make the church as sturdy as possible. Beams were made of heavy pine from nearby Figueroa Mountain. Above the sanctuary, the ceiling was made of painted wood.

## DECORATION

Like the other missions before it, Mission Santa Inés had a layout in the shape of a quadrangle. This meant that all of the buildings formed a square shape. Neophytes decorated the insides of the buildings with painting materials utilized by the Chumash for centuries: the rocks and minerals that helped them make paint for their pictographs. They also added herbs, roots, and berries to create new colors. These were used to paint decorations of vines, baskets, vases, and even marble.

The floors of the church were constructed of handmade tiles created by the neophytes. Some of these tiles still have the footprints of children and animals in them. It seems that they had stepped on the tiles before they were completely dry!

# GENERAL FEATURES OF THE MISSION

Next to the church was a cemetery. And beside it, on one side of the square, stood the friars' rooms, offices, living and guest quarters, and a monjerío. Workshops, barns, stables, and warehouses formed the other sides of the square. All the members of the mission community would meet in the center of the square where a fountain stood. It was there that they celebrated festivals, played games, sang songs, and danced.

A brick building, used for bathing and washing, stood in front of the mission. On one side were the gardens and orchards, and on the other were the huts and tiled houses where the neophyte families lived.

The mission received its water supply from the mountains. First the community dug ditches, and then they lined them with waterproof pipes. The pipes carried water from the mountains to the mission grounds.

Once the church was finished, the community at Mission Santa Inés grew quickly. Herds of cattle and flocks of sheep increased. The mission was built in a beautiful valley that gave the mission its nickname "the Hidden Gem of the Missions." Still, Mission Santa Inés had few visitors. This was because it was far from the main roads and difficult to reach. For this reason, whenever visitors came, the friars and neophytes welcomed them with singing, dancing, and celebrating. Everyone at the mission would gather at the door to greet them.

# 6
# Daily Life at the Mission

Life for the neophytes at Mission Santa Inés was the same for those living in the other missions. The bell was an important part of the mission system, and Mission Santa Inés had three. One was cast in 1804, another in 1808, and the final one in 1818. Each morning at sunrise, the church bells woke those living at the mission and called them to church. After morning prayers and Mass, they sat down to a breakfast of *atole*—porridge made of corn that was served during most mealtimes. This was followed by morning chores.

## WORK AND CHORES

At Mission Santa Inés, men built mission structures, worked in the fields, and learned many trades such as leather making, shoemaking, and blacksmithing. The women and girls, on the other hand, learned to weave in the Spanish tradition using large looms and spent much of their day making blankets, sheets, tablecloths, towels, and napkins. They also made elaborate tapestries to hang on the walls of the mission and performed other chores such as assisting in the kitchens or cleaning. Boys usually spent their mornings listening to the friars teach lessons

on Christianity or did chores of their own. The friars taught the male neophytes to read and write in both Spanish and Latin. This was thought to be important because then the neophytes and non-mission Native people could communicate with the friars and better understand the Bible.

At noon the bells interrupted everyone's work for the midday meal. This was usually *pozole*, cornmeal eaten with beans, vegetables, or meat. The neophytes then took a *siesta*—an afternoon nap—until 2 p.m. before starting work again.

The men spent the rest of the day building or working in the fields. They herded cattle, horses, and sheep. When harvest season was over, they made adobe bricks or tiles, which would be used for new buildings. The women would continue their day by weaving, preparing food in the kitchens, and doing laundry.

## TIME TO RELAX

At sundown, the bells ended the workday and the evening meal was prepared. After dinner, there was little time for games and other pastimes before the bells rang for evening prayers. One of

**This is a depiction of a band taught by Fray Duran at Mission San Jose. During festival times or special occasions, everyone would gather to celebrate with music and dancing.**

the games the Chumash played was *tikauwich,* or shinny. It likened to an early version of hockey and was played on a large open field with two teams.

No one worked on Sundays or holidays. On these days, the neophytes were free to do what they liked after the morning Mass and afternoon prayers. They were sometimes allowed to visit their villages, but only if they had received permission from the missionaries.

The mission was dedicated to Saint Agnes, so the *Día de Santa Inés,* or Saint Agnes's Feast Day, was one of the most important festivals at the mission. It was celebrated with horseracing and bullfights on a large open square.

## GROWING UP AT THE MISSION

The lives of neophyte boys and girls at the missions were very different. At around age eleven, the girls had to leave their mothers and live and work at the monjerío. Once they finished their work, they were allowed to visit their families. However, at night their dormitories were locked and protected by soldiers to make sure that no one got in or out. Until they were married, girls and women in the monjerío lived under strict supervision.

The neophyte boys, on the other hand, were not locked in at night or forced to stay in during the day. The friars trained the boys to become bell ringers, sing in the choir, or play the violin. They enjoyed much more freedom, and for that reason lived happier lives at the mission.

# A NEW WAY OF LIVING

The daily schedule was very different from the life the neophytes once knew. When the missionaries first came to them, the neophytes could not foresee that they would lose their freedom, be forced to give up their way of life, and be kept inside the missions. To some, it felt as if they were imprisoned.

Many of the neophytes grew unhappy and tried to run away, but the soldiers would go after them and bring them back to the mission. Those who returned were severely punished. Other neophytes, however, remained willingly. The missions did try to give the neophytes protection from traders and other settlers who had little regard for the lives of the neophytes, but their methods of caring for them were not always kind.

The friars wanted to protect the neophytes from cruelty of others, but they were simply unable to. Some friars themselves became violent to the Native people over time. The cruel actions of many Europeans and the diseases that they brought with them would harm and upset many Native people.

# 7
# Troubling Times

The damage caused by the 1812 earthquake paled in comparison to that of revolts and the spread of disease. Mission numbers declined as the work continued, for many different reasons.

## ILLNESS AND EPIDEMICS

Illnesses such as measles, chicken pox, and smallpox were unknown to the Native people before Europeans arrived. When they did, they unknowingly brought with them life-threatening diseases. The Native population had not built up immunity to fight the sicknesses, thus many died. The number of neophytes and indigenous people in the area drastically declined. In the early 1800s, an epidemic, thought to be measles, swept through the Alta California missions, causing neophytes and Native Californians to die in great numbers. Mission Santa Inés suffered losses during this time, too, and again in the 1820s when a diphtheria epidemic took its toll.

**Joseph Chapman was once a pirate who later married a Native woman and worked at Mission Santa Inés.**

## PIRATES

Another problem affecting missions along California's coast were attacks in 1818 by a pirate named Hippolyte de Bouchard. De Bouchard was a French-born man who worked for Argentina. He was determined to terrorize the settlers in Spain's territories and threaten soldiers at the presidios. While Mission Santa Inés did not suffer directly at the hands of the pirates, it did have a person of significance at the mission: Joseph Chapman. Chapman had worked under de Bouchard and played a part in upsetting the missions and soldiers of Alta California's coast. However, after plundering, or taking by force, a ranch near Santa Barbara, Chapman and others were captured and imprisoned. After his release, Chapman became a new man, eventually married into the Catholic faith, and became a handyman at Santa Inés. The mission benefited from his skills in planting vineyards and in construction. In 1821, Chapman built the mission's fulling mill, which was used to treat wool so that it was less scratchy.

## PASQUALA

There is a legend in the mission's history about a girl named Pasquala who saved Santa Inés from the Tulares. Pasquala was a neophyte who came from the Yokut tribe and had lived with her parents at Mission Santa Inés for some time. While working in the fields one day in 1824, her father was attacked and killed, and she and her mother were taken by the Tulares. Her mother was also killed. When Pasquala learned of what the Tulares would do to the

**The year 1824 saw revolts occur at missions Santa Inés, Santa Bárbara, and La Purísima Concepción.**

mission, she escaped and ran for days over rocky ground until she found lead friar Fray Francisco Xavier Uría, who prepared the soldiers to attack. Though it is said she died shortly after, rumor has it that she was buried on the mission grounds.

# FIGHTING AND REVOLT

Another serious problem for missions was the fear of revolt. Conditions and treatment of the neophytes led to more neophytes trying to escape. The friars did their best to soothe tensions and keep people happy, but soon the abuse from soldiers and unhappiness became overwhelming. Following Mexico's independence from Spain (1821), a rebellion led by neophytes swept over Missions Santa Inés, La Purísima Concepción, and Santa Bárbara in February 1824. It was the most successful uprising of neophytes in the history of the missions.

The trouble had been brewing since the start of Mexico's war for independence from Spain in 1810. Spain spent so much of its resources fighting this war that it could no longer support the missions, as they had once done. As a result, the mission soldiers did not receive their wages and supplies regularly. The soldiers then depended on the missions for food, clothing, and other supplies. The neophytes had to work harder and harder, without pay, to support the soldiers. To make matters worse, the soldiers mistreated the workers. Of course, this angered the Chumash people. After independence was won, the neophytes worked for the Mexican army and conditions worsened.

Then in February 1824, Chumash neophytes from Mission La Purísima Concepción visited Mission Santa Inés. While there, one of the La Purísima neophytes was whipped by a Spanish soldier. The Chumash were outraged. As a result, a thousand neophytes attacked Mission Santa Inés with bows, arrows, and fire. The neophytes took their anger out on the soldiers and not at the friars, who had been kind to them. The friars were treated with respect and affection, and the neophytes wanted no harm to come to them. Some of the friars, though, decided to leave, fearful for their lives.

The fighting at Mission Santa Inés went on for less than a week. The conflict spread to Mission La Purísima Concepción and Santa Bárbara. It was only when soldiers from the Santa Barbara presidio arrived that the fighting was put to an end. In the aftermath of the conflict, several people were dead and many buildings were burned beyond repair. Mission La Purísima Concepción suffered the worst damage, and its neophyte population decreased after the uprising.

# 8
# Secularization

While Mexico's independence was celebrated by the people who had tried so hard to win it, the switch from power—from Spain to Mexico—had a disastrous effect on the California missions. Steps taken in the 1820s to 1840s threatened the mission system and affected the lives of all involved in it.

## SECULARIZATION ACTS

In 1834, the Mexican government passed **secularization** laws. These laws meant that the missions no longer belonged to the Catholic Church and missionaries could no longer convert Native tribes to Christianity. Instead the missions would only be used to preserve the faith of Christianity as churches for the community. The friars living there had to pledge an oath of allegiance to Mexico, otherwise they were sent back to Spain and replaced by Mexican priests.

The missions were turned into *pueblos* and **parishes**, and the neophytes were free to leave. The plan was for one-half of the land to be divided among the neophytes and the other half to be used for agriculture and other common needs. Instead, the land was illegally given or sold to Mexican ranchers. Many neophytes did not understand the concept of land ownership. They thought the land should be for everyone. To them, owning a piece of land was as ridiculous as owning a piece of sky.

Many neophytes returned to their mountain villages or went to work at ranches for little more than room and board. Others remained behind because they had nowhere else to go. Their villages no longer existed. Their own ways of hunting and gathering were lost. Their language and ceremonial rituals were forgotten. Without their own culture, many neophytes did not have the means to live better lives in freedom than they had lived at the missions.

**Ten years after its secularization, Mission Santa Inés became a seminary.**

# SECULARIZATION OF MISSION SANTA INÉS

Mission Santa Inés was secularized in 1834. Many of the neophytes left, unhappy with the way the Mexican government treated them. In 1844, Mission Santa Inés became a seminary, or priest school, called Our Lady of Refuge. It remained operating until 1881. In the twentieth century the mission would undergo restoration and preservation that would transform it into the mission heritage site known today.

Today Mission Santa Inés is a national landmark and popular tourist destination.

# 9
# Mission Santa Inés Today

Following the closing of Our Lady of Refuge, the mission grounds focused on the needs of the community and continued ministering to the families in the area as the local church. In 1884, the mission priest, Father Michael Lynch, invited a family, the Donahues, to live at the mission. Mr. Donahue was a carpenter, and he and his sons carried out the first repairs on the buildings.

## RESTORATION

In 1904, a major, twenty-year restoration project began under Father Alexander Buckler, the head priest at the church at that time. He had help from his niece, Mamie Goulet, who devoted those twenty years not only to restoring the mission's artifacts but also the unique collection of friars' vestments, or robes, that are on display at the mission today. Gathered mostly from Baja California missions, these vestments were made from fine materials such as silk, satins, and damasks, and date from the early fifteenth century to the eighteenth century.

In 1911 the mission suffered heavy rains, which caused the bell tower to collapse. However, it was quickly restored with the help of settlers in the new town of Solvang nearby. In 1924, the mission was given over to the Capuchin **Franciscans**, who tend to the grounds and care for the church today.

## THE MISSION TODAY

Today Mission Santa Inés is one of the best-preserved Spanish missions in the United States. The low, flatlands on which its orchards grew are now fields of wheat. The pipes that the neophytes laid so that the mission could receive water from the mountains can still be seen. On a Chumash reservation nearby, descendants of the mission's neophytes carry on the job of rediscovering and preserving their culture.

Some of the buildings constructed by the friars and neophytes remain: the adobe church, which was rebuilt in 1817; the monjerío; and the neophyte village. Inside the buildings, examples of the neophytes' fine arts and crafts can be viewed.

Today, these restored buildings are in such excellent condition that the National Landmark Committee has made Mission Santa Inés a national landmark. It will be preserved for future generations to visit, so they can learn about the lives of the friars and neophytes of the California missions.

Mission Santa Inés and the rest of the mission system in California changed the way hundreds of Native people lived and viewed their world. While this had an impact on and damaged many cultures, the system also introduced many techniques that make up California today, such as farming and architecture. Overall, the missions offer unique insight into one of the most transformative periods of California's past.

# 10
# Make Your Own Mission Model

**To make your own model of the Santa Inés mission, you will need:**

- Foam Core board
- glue
- greenery
- miniature bell
- paintbrush
- pencil
- red paint
- ruler
- scissors
- wire
- wire mesh

## DIRECTIONS

**Adult supervision is suggested.**

**Step 1:** Cut eight pieces of wire mesh that measure 12 " × 2 " (30.5 × 5 cm) to form the base and roof of the mission.

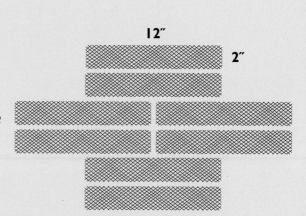

**Step 2:** Use the wire to sew together four of the mesh pieces into a flat square. Repeat this step to form another square.

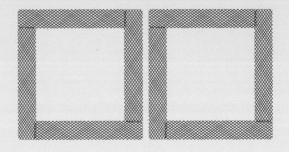

**Step 3:** Cut two pieces of mesh to measure 12" × 3" (30.5 × 7.6 cm). These will form the sides of the mission.

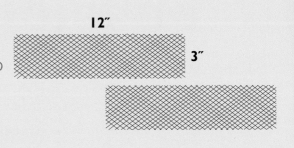

**Step 4:** Sew one of the 12" × 3" (30.5 × 7.6 cm) mesh rectangles perpendicular to one 12" (30.5 cm) side of the base. Attach the other 12" × 3" (30.5 × 7.6 cm) mesh rectangle to the opposite side.

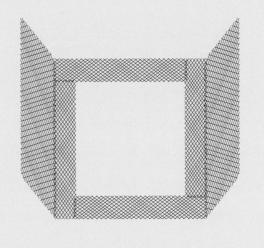

**Step 5:** Cut out eight pieces of mesh measuring 2" × 3" (5 cm × 7.6 cm). Bend the edges of each piece to make them look like 3" (7.6 cm) columns.

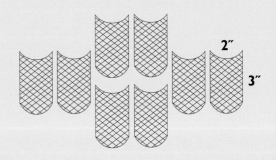

**Step 6:** Attach one of the columns to the left side of the mission front. Attach another column 6" (15.2 cm) from the other side. Attach two more columns equal distances from each other.

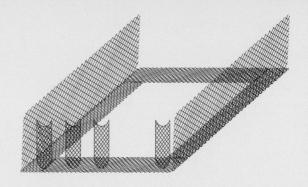

**Step 7:** On the back of the mission, attach the other four columns an equal distance from each other.

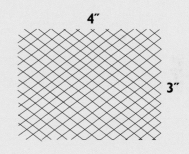

**Step 8:** Cut out a piece of mesh measuring 4" × 3" (10.1 × 7.6 cm). This will be the front of the church.

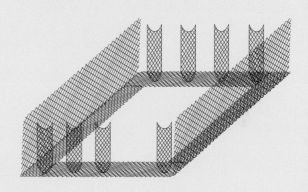

**Step 9:** Cut out the bell wall from the wire mesh. This shape should measure about 3" × 6" (7.6 × 15.2 cm). Decorate the top of the bell wall and glue a wire cross on top.

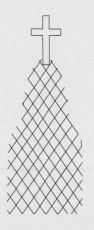

**Step 10:** Attach the church front and the bell wall to the right side of the mission base. The bell wall should be the farthest to the right. Using a piece of wire, attach a miniature bell to the bell wall.

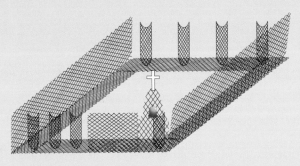

**Step 11:** Using wire, sew the pieces of the roof onto the mission.

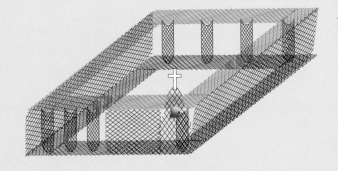

**Step 12:** Paint the roof red. Allow it to dry.

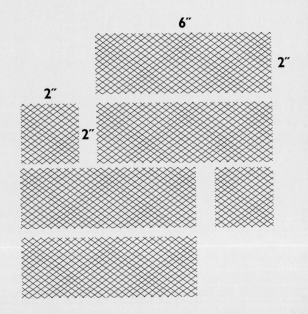

**Step 13:** To make the workshops, cut out two mesh pieces measuring 2" × 2" (5 × 5 cm) and four pieces that measure 6" × 2" (15.2 × 5 cm).

**Step 14:** Use wire to sew these pieces into a box shape.

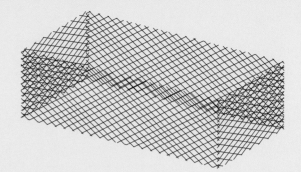

**Step 15:** Using the Foam Core board as a base, place all buildings on top of it. Decorate the mission with flowers and trees.

**The model of Mission Santa Inés when it is completed.**

# Key Dates in Mission History

**1492**  Christopher Columbus reaches the West Indies

**1542**  Cabrillo's expedition to California

**1602**  Sebastián Vizcaíno sails to California

**1713**  Fray Junípero Serra is born

**1769**  Founding of San Diego de Alcalá

**1770**  Founding of San Carlos Borroméo del Río Carmelo

**1771**  Founding of San Antonio de Padua and
San Gabriel Arcángel

**1772**  Founding of San Luis Obispo de Tolosa

**1775-76**  Founding of San Juan Capistrano

**1776**  Founding of San Francisco de Asís

**1776**  Declaration of Independence is signed

| 1777 | Founding of Santa Clara de Asís |
| 1782 | Founding of San Buenaventura |
| 1784 | Fray Serra dies |
| 1786 | Founding of Santa Bárbara |
| 1787 | Founding of La Purísima Concepción |
| 1791 | Founding of Santa Cruz and Nuestra Señora de la Soledad |
| 1797 | Founding of San José, San Juan Bautista, San Miguel Arcángel, and San Fernando Rey de España |
| 1798 | Founding of San Luis Rey de Francia |
| 1804 | Founding of Santa Inés |
| 1817 | Founding of San Rafael Arcángel |
| 1823 | Founding of San Francisco Solano |
| 1833 | Mexico passes Secularization Act |
| 1848 | Gold found in northern California |
| 1850 | California becomes the thirty-first state |

# Glossary

**adobe (uh-DOH-bee)** Sun-dried bricks made of straw, mud, and sometimes manure.

**amulet (AM-yoo-let)** An item worn to bring good luck or to keep away bad luck.

**colonists (KAH-luh-nists)** People who settle in a new land.

**conquistador (kon-KEE-stuh-dor)** An adventurer or conqueror, especially one of the Spanish conquerors of the New World in the 16th century; usually a soldier who comes to a country to take control, or conquer, it.

**convert (kon-VERT)** To cause someone to change beliefs or religions.

**dialect (DYE-ah-lekt)** An accent, or a different way of speaking a certain language.

**empire (EM-pyr)** A large area under one ruler.

**Franciscan (fran-SIS-kan)** Friars belonging to the Franciscan order, a part of the Catholic Church started by Saint Francis in 1209.

**friar (FRY-ur)** A brother in a communal religious order. Friars can also be priests.

**martyr (MAR-ter)** A person who is put to death or made to suffer because of his religious beliefs.

**neophyte (NEE-oh-fyt)** A person who has converted to another religion.

**parish (PAR-ish)** An area with its own church and minister or priest.

**secularization (sehk-yoo-luh-rih-ZAY-shun)** A process by

which the mission lands were
made to be nonreligious.

**settlement (SEH-tul-ment)** A
small village or group of houses.

**thatch (THACH)** Tule or reeds
used to build a roof or covering.

# Pronunciation Guide

atole (ah-TOL-ay)

Chumash (CHOO-mahsh)

El Camino Real (El kah-MEE-no RAY-al)

fray (FRAY)

monjerío (mohn-hay-REE-oh)

pozole (poh-ZOHL-ay)

pueblos (PWAY-blohs)

siesta (see-EHS-tah)

# Find Out More

For more information on Mission Santa Inés and the California missions, check out these books, videos, and websites:

## BOOKS

Gendell, Megan. *The Spanish Missions of California*. New York, NY: Scholastic, 2010.

Gibson, Karen Bush. *Native American History for Kids*. Chicago, IL: Chicago Review Press, 2010.

Rosinsky, Natalie M. *California Ranchos*. Capstone: Edina, MN, 2006.

Weber, Matt. *California's Missions A to Z*. San Francisco, CA: 121 Publications, 2010.

## VIDEO

**"Missions of California: Father Junípero Serra"**
Produced by Chip Taylor Productions
Discover the historical importance of Franciscan missionary Junípero Serra, who is considered the founder of the California missions. Learn how his leadership proved critical to the founding of California, opening an important page to the history of the American West. Check your local library for availability or order by calling 1-800-876-CHIP.

# WEBSITES

**California Missions Resource Center**

www.missionscalifornia.com/keyfacts/santa-ines.html

View an 1824 map of the California missions. Explore an interactive timeline noting the important events in the founding and development of the region the Spanish called Alta California between 1768 and 1853.

**Mission Tour**

www.missiontour.org/santaines/history.htm

Learn more about the history of Mission Santa Inés through a virtual tour. Explore the mission front, museum, cemetery, church, garden, and lavendería.

**Santa Ynez Band of Chumash Indians**

www.santaynezchumash.org/history.html

Learn more about the Chumash people, who once numbered in the tens of thousands and lived along the coast of California. Explore Chumash culture and the Santa Ynez Reservation in Santa Barbara County.

# Index